ARYANNA KONNOR

CUSTOMER SUCCESS

The Essential Guide On How to Deal With Difficult Customers, Learn Effective Customer Service Techniques and Strategies on How You Can Win Difficult Customers

Descrierea CIP a Bibliotecii Naţionale a României
ARYANNA KONNOR
  CUSTOMER SUCCESS. The Essential Guide On How to Deal With Difficult Customers, Learn Effective Customer Service Techniques and Strategies on How You Can Win Difficult Customers / Aryanna Konnor – Bucharest: Editura My Ebook, 2021
  ISBN

ARYANNA KONNOR

CUSTOMER SUCCESS

The Essential Guide On How to Deal With Difficult Customers, Learn Effective Customer Service Techniques and Strategies on How You Can Win Difficult Customers

My Ebook Publishing House
Bucharest, 2021

TABLE OF CONTENTS

INTRODUCTION

If you're in business you'll understand more than anyone else that business is not about product features, benefits, revenue, or anything so stuffy and businesslike. It's about people.

The trouble with that rather heartwarming statement is that people can be real pains in the butt. (Were you expecting a very politically correct report here?)

Ask any poor unfortunate who has manned the customer service desk for any business, and I daresay in any place in the world, and they could dine out on the stories they have to tell you.

Dealing with the public is often something that scares people. Sometimes it can add to their day when that extra little personal contact leaves them feeling like they've been helpful and served a purpose. But there are those times when someone who's obviously on a mission to destroy your soul will appear in a sulfur- scented puff of smoke.

What makes these difficult people a double blow to you or your employee is that contrary to long held opinion, people don't judge themselves on their pay or status as much as might be assumed. The philosopher Maslow arrived at the idea that people behave according to a hierarchy of needs which they need fulfilled.

They are:

- Physiological – food and water
- Safety – in our ancestor's time this meant getting away from sabre toothed tigers Social – the need to have friends
- Esteem – the need to be thought highly of
- Self-actualization – this is self knowledge, spirituality and religion

The problem with Maslow's hierarchy, as you might imagine is that people tend to want all of those things and all at the same time. This is contrary to Maslow's idea that only after achieving one level do we look to the next.

But we know now that people don't graduate from one set of needs to another – they try to attain most or all of these needs simultaneously.

Studies have shown that people often yearn more for social esteem than financial reward. They want to feel that as a human being, they provide a valuable contribution to society.

Which means that actual money and status generally don't compare to a feeling of being useful – of having a purpose.

So when one of these red faced, angry customers start to tear away at that sense of value, it can be emotionally devastating.

That's why it's important to understand what your customer expects of you. And more importantly, what you should expect of your customer. It's all about customer service.

Customer service has evolved over the years. When it began, the process involved a trip to the shop where an item was bought. Then in 1876 the telephone was invented. At first their use was limited, but as they grew in popularity they enabled customers to contact the stores they shopped at directly to look for customer service.

When the '60s arrived, so too did call centers which really took off in the '70s – and are as reviled today as they were popular back then.

There was a short gap between the launch of touch tone dialing ("please press #2 for customer service") in 1962 and the invention of 1-800 numbers in 1967.

Interactive voice responses automated customer service in the late '70s and early '80s.

It was as far back as the late '80s when call centers were outsourced, and so began their slow lingering slide into a source of utter frustration on the part of many consumers. But we have more technological advances in customer service to go, just yet.

In the '90s the emergence of the Internet brought the ability to use email and live chat support to the world.

Now – we can look for customer service through a wide variety of resources at our fingertips. Almost none of the old forms have died out. They just became more sophisticated over time. With the exception of call centers.

Social media is now the form of communication that approximately 60% of the population has used to seek customer support.

Yet despite all the advances in customer support, we still face many of the same issues – when customers and customer support are brought out of isolated existence and forced to meet.

THE POWER OF CUSTOMER SERVICE

Customer service is what ultimately makes or breaks a company. If it's done well, it will establish a fantastic reputation that will spread goodwill towards the company by word of mouth.

Done badly though, and the results can be catastrophic.

According to an American Express survey in 2011, 78% of consumers have abandoned a transaction or not followed through on an intended purchase due to poor customer service.

And data from "Understanding Customers" by Ruby Newell-Legner indicates that only 4% of dissatisfied customers ever voice their feelings. (Though that figure may seem much higher to you!)

But get it right and your business can not only shine as an example to others, but make a lot more money while you do so.

A White House Office of Consumer Affairs report states that returning customers are worth an average of 10 times their initial purchase. They also don't cost as much to retain as new customers cost to acquire.

With these facts in mind, let's take a look at the world of customer service.

Customer Service Heroes

What is customer service, or more accurately, what does it mean to you?

Customer service is one of those phrases that appear everywhere – Yelp, FourSquare, Google Reviews – and it's one of the things most often remarked upon by consumers. But what exactly does customer service mean?

The term itself is rather abstract. What may be a deal breaker in how a vendor treats me, may be something you find completely acceptable – maybe even business as usual.

One thing is sure, though. We all know great customer service when we experience it.

And those who offer great customer service? They become almost superstars in the eyes of many, creating strong business brands and powerful personas that seem to spread their stories far and wide without effort.

Harry Selfridge

Customer service fascinates consumers when it is approached with the right attitude. Just look at the success of the TV program Mister Selfridge, in which an American businessman from Chicago opens up a department store in London, UK.

Selfridge doesn't have the necessary money to even get the store built, he lacks the finances to pay his staff, and worse – he has some very strange ideas about doing business. Ideas like allowing customers choose from a variety of items vulgarly left out on display rather than kept hidden away and recommended to them only when they gave specific details about the products they wanted.

All because his motto is to give the customer what they want. In other words, by placing the customer first. It was Selfridge who coined the proverb that drives many businesses service department policies (for right or wrong): "The customer is always right."

The idea that a store owner might be a rebel for ensuring that a customer might choose from several products or be the one to decide what best fit their taste may seem like a bit of a joke to us. Nowadays that's business as usual. But in London, 1910, this was highly unusual.

Slefridge's store remains an iconic part of modern London, and the American's influence changed the face of British retail. It is the only store to be named The Best Department Store in the World 3 times, and Selfridges management describe the store as a "shopping experience that promises to surprise, amaze and amuse its customers by delivering extraordinary customer experiences".

With that as a store description, how can it possibly fail? But there's more to Selfridges customer service than a fanciful description that could be straight from a Harry Potter novel.

In 2015 Selfridges added a tax refund lounge for its international visitors, 2 libraries and a meditation lounge and a theatre ticket booking desk. It tripled the size of its customer service area. How's that for taking its customers seriously?

Here are 3 quotes from Harry Gordon Selfridge that illustrate his forward thinking and leadership in customer service:

"People will sit up and take notice of you if you will sit up and take notice of what makes them sit up and take notice."

"The customer is always right." "Give the lady what she wants."

This kind of customer-centric approach is common these days. "The customer is always right" has been overused to the point of cliché. But to say that people take notice when you take notice of them is still a fairly forward thinking idea.

Dale Carnegie

Another great businessman of our time was Dale Carnegie. He was a man so focused on the customer that his writing on the subject has become some of the most influential business writing in the world.

Personally, I think he ought to have chosen a different title for "How to Win Friends and Influence People." I can't imagine anyone of a shy disposition wanting to buy that over the counter. And they didn't have Kindles back then.

Carnegie was another American. A writer and lecturer, he was the founder of many courses on self improvement. He worked as a salesman for Nebraskan company; Armour & Co.

An avid public speaker and teacher, he wrote pamphlets about his ideas on becoming more self confident and interacting better with people. He was of the opinion that public speaking was the best way to increase self-esteem.

The most likely reason that Carnegie's biggest bestseller (How to Win Friends and Influence People, which has sold over

10 million books in various languages) was so well received is that it lays out what Carnegie laid out as simple rules that made sense for anyone who wished to achieve success in interpersonal relationships.

Warren Buffet accredits much of his success to finding a copy of the book on his grandfather's shelf when he was a 15 year old kid who found it difficult to fit in at school.

Carnegie's rules for behavior aren't big news anymore, but here are some of his quotes that should be immortalized on any customer service desk:

"Any fool can criticize, condemn, and complain — and most fools do." "Abilities wither under criticism; they blossom under encouragement."

"The only way on earth to influence other people is to talk about what *they* want and show them how to get it."

"A man convinced against his will is of the same opinion still."

"Begin by emphasizing — and keep on emphasizing — the things on which you agree."

Carnegie's brilliance was for seeing to the heart of what makes people tick – and that skill was one that people wanted to learn. A poor farm boy from Missouri, his first class was made up of 9 engineers in New York, and by 2012, a hundred years later, 8 million people in 83 countries and speaking 30 different languages had gone through his training.

The Dale Carnegie training method is still widely popular in business circles even today.

To learn more about Dale Carnegie's courses visit http://www.dalecarnegie.com/www.dalecarnegie.com

Nordstrom

In later days, Nordstrom became the modern leaders in great customer service.

This time founded by a Swedish man who left home in 1887 to open a shoe store in New York, with $5 to his name.

Nowadays, the management at Nordstrom understand that the store offers products at higher price points than their competitors and decide to differentiate themselves with customer service that excels.

That's the reasoning behind Nordstrom staff offering to gift wrap a customer's purchase, even though he had bought it at Macy's. And it's why one staff member took a customer's car keys and went to heat up his car in the snow outside the store while the customer was paying for his purchases.

Other initiatives employees have taken to ensure great customer satisfaction are:

- paying customer's parking tickets
- accepting returns without question or hesitation
- lending money to customers
- sending tailors to customer's homes

And then there's what might otherwise have been thought of as an urban legend if it weren't vouched for as true in the book, The Nordstrom Way (available on Amazon): a shopper decided to return a pair of snow tires – even though Nordstrom didn't sell snow tires, the cashier refunded the cost of the snow tires to the customer.

Whether this is actually true or not, it might explain their decision to expand from shoes into other goods. Regardless, it demonstrates an absolute focus on becoming known for excellent customer service.

There's no doubt in anyone's mind that Nordstrom offers excellent customer service.

What We Can Learn from these Customer Service Heroes

You may notice that as these great men entered business they made up their own rules and those rules always put the customer first in whatever methods of selling they employed.

The golden rule of all business is to serve others. When you find someone with a problem and solve it for them, then you have a business. You can become a customer service super hero by:

- helping your customer make the right decision about the product they purchase (make sure it effectively solves their problem)

- making your offer the best it can be (a product or service that over delivers for a price that's reasonable)

- educating your customer on how to use the product (so that they are happy they understand how to get the best from it)

- being patient with them when they have a complaint or query

- adding some personality to the business transaction (people like to deal with people, not automatons that spew out pre-scripted replies designed to fob off an inconvenient complaint)

If only it were easy to offer such great customer service. We'd all love to be known as the Harry Selfridge or Nordstrom of our industry - but we forget that while this idea is perfect in isolation, customer service often doesn't survive an encounter with customers.

TYPES OF DIFFICULT CUSTOMERS

How many different types of difficult customer are there? You may as well ask how many words do the igloos have for snow? (2, 5 or 9 9 – depending on who you talk to). But there are as many different types of difficult customers, or difficult behaviors that business owners, entrepreneurs and customer service staff commonly have to confront, as there are different types of human being.

The customers you are likely to meet will vary according to your role – entrepreneur, employee, or business owner. And with each level of responsibility comes a different stress.

Difficult Customers You Will Meet

Death, taxes, and difficult customers. 3 Things you can be certain of in life.

Often, how you react will determine the outcome of your interaction with a difficult customer. Which means you will need to master several different skills to adapt according to the situation.

Let's take a look at the several different types of customers and how to deal with them.

It's safe to say that different customer behaviors can often be so similar they deserve their own customer avatars based on them.

The Aggressive One

This guy just doesn't care that the mistake is his. He didn't read the product description, and was only half aware of what it did before he bought it. But he knows it doesn't do what he thought it did and now he's calling you and your staff incompetent. He doesn't want to talk about it either – just wants to vent his anger.

The product could be anything from a dishwasher to a bank loan to a hotel booking. What's important to recognize is the absolute lack of interest in discussion.

How to deal with the aggressive one:

Fault is irrelevant, whether it's yours or his. Just don't start matching his anger with your own angry response. Ignore nasty words and wait till he has vented all his anger and is deflated. Then, remaining calm and polite, ask how you may rectify the situation. If it involves a refund and the loss of an aggressive client – cut him loose and move on.

The High Priority One

This lady doesn't care for queuing – she's been done badly by, and she knows her needs are greater than everyone else's. She'll skip the queue (or demand prioritization and faster service online).

How to deal with the high priority one:

While a prompt response is what you should aim for in all customer service, this is one case where referring the customer to one of your colleagues is definitely allowed.

Solo operator? Then have a support desk created so that you can issue support tickets. This places a little anonymity between you and the customer in question.

The One Who Knows More than You

There's always someone who reckons they could run your business better than you do.

Their sentences often start with "Don't you know how to…"

This customer will insist they know what they are doing when they buy a product that's all wrong for them – despite your best efforts at persuading them otherwise.

They're also great at pointing out the errors in your knowledge about how a product or service works – and how your competitors do things differently.

How to deal with the one who knows more than you:

This customer's ego is top of their personal priority list. They don't just want your admiration (and that of all onlookers), they *need* it.

You can take advantage by challenging their perception of the status quo. The font type Comic Sans still gets used on websites (yes, even now in the 21st Century) when website owners should know better. It's outdated, horrible to read for site visitors and just screams "amateur, don't take me seriously."

You need to find your customer's Comic Sans and point it out to them, but then follow up with an alternative product solution and explain why it is more in line with their professional or expert status.

A Harvard Business Review report states that sales people who challenge their customers are much more likely to make a sale – even outperforming those who chose relationship building as a sales vehicle.

The trick is to follow the challenge with an assertion that supports your customer's belief in their own self value.

The One Who Never Says a Good Thing about Anything or Anyone

This guy notices every speck of dirt on the drinking glass, every stain on the carpet, every crack in your product's screen, every sloppy, half-hearted mismanaged aspect of your badly run business.

They're a real pleasure to have around. Not.

How to deal with the ones who never have a good thing to say: Don't even try.

There's nothing you can do with this customer, so don't even try. Just apologize. Apologize for your product, your lack of service, for the fact it's a Monday. Just apologize.

But whatever you do, don't offer an excuse – or any time of reasoning.

Deal with him by solving his issue as quickly as possible so that you can move him on and out of your hair, but don't offer anything that will resemble the opening of a discussion.

Let this know-it-all leave with the form idea that he is correct and you know it.

The One who Never Complains to Your Face

I'm sure if you have ever worked with a team of people, you'll already have come across this person.

When asked if there's anything that can be done to help them they shake their heads demurely and pointedly stare at the ground. They're inoffensive from the start.

They won't tell you what they want, exactly, because they are afraid of being demanding. And the more you try to pin down an accurate answer from them, the more they squirm like a worm on a hook.

How to deal with the silent squirmers:

You have no choice but to ask questions at every opportunity. If she won't be explicit in her needs when she is buying a product or service, break it down into parts.

"Would you like one with a red or a blue cover?"

"Should it have wheels or do you prefer a stationery one?" "Is it intended for indoor or outdoor use?"

At each step along the way, try to point out what the pros and cons of each decision are so that you are educating her about the final product as you guide her decision. In that way she can't complain that she is unhappy with her choice for any reason.

DEALING WITH DIFFICULT CUSTOMERS

Why not just round 'em up and chuck 'em all in a lake? After all, if people are going to be downright disagreeable, why should you really go to the bother of bowing and scraping to these people?

Sure, you can feel that way. But consider these points:

- on average, it takes a further 12 positive experiences to outweigh just 1 bad one

- over twice as many people are more likely to listen to stories about bad customer service than good (you may feel that this reflects on a lot of negativity in people – but it's often a case of people wishing to educate themselves about avoiding bad experiences based on those of other people)

- It is approximately 7 times more expensive to gain a new customer compared to keep a current one

- 60% of Americans would rather try a new service if they believe it will offer a better customer service

It becomes quite clear that not creating a positive experience for customers can have a dramatic impact on your bottom line. So let's talk about how you can deal with these monsters ;-)

A.K.A. How Not to Go Home with a Headache after Work and Start a Fight with Your Partner

First – if you're a freelancer or a small business and are involved directly with your customers, you have more control over how you deal with your customers.

Here's a shock tactic that will work: fire your worst customers.

Not what you expected to hear in advice on dealing with people, right? But think about it: if you have a small number of customers who insist on being difficult – and this bit is important: they don't bring in the majority of your income – then you should consider make excuses as to your availability and

For some reason your customer may not believe that you are providing the customer service they are worthy of.

You Can't Avoid All Confrontation

While it's kind of fun to consider all the different types of difficult customers and give them names – you need a process that can be adapted to every customer.

Even if you could hand pick your own customers, the odds are that you would still end up in a position where customer service is required. In that case, let's take a look at what you can do to survive the situation.

Remove yourself from the situation.

No – don't run away! But when you adopt a customer mindset, the first thing you need to do is remove your feelings. Specifically those feelings that tell you lies – like it's your fault the product doesn't work as it should. Emotions other than empathy do not serve a purpose in customer care.

That means setting aside your feelings about the product too. If it's one you love and use yourself you may not be able to see the same flaw that your customer sees.

Men and women in relationships argue all the time because the woman just wants someone to vent to and the man wants to fix the problem (in general terms). Most of us have learned that from the copious amounts of self help books we're encouraged to read. But in this case, the emphasis is definitely on solving the problem.

It's the problem that is causing the customer to be difficult. You and he may have a completely different viewpoint – but it's the fault with the product or service (in the eyes of the customer) that becomes the focal point for the issue.

Resolve that problem and the focal point for the disagreement will be removed.

Listen Actively

While this will be much easier to accomplish when you don't feel as if it's a personal battle, another trait you will need to acquire is that of an active listener.

Active listening means you are paying full attention to your customer. You are internalizing their issue and doing your best to understand why they feel the way they do – or what you can do to fix the issue – not going through a mental rolodex of rote replies to find which answer suits this situation.

I recall when working as a junior technician in the service department for one of the first mobile phone companies to offer a drop-in service desk for phone repairs, overhearing a jovial customers mention that with all the faults in his phone, it must surely have been a "Monday morning" phone. In other words, a phone that someone created after an exciting weekend that left them tired and likely hungover on Monday morning, and completely lacking interest in what they were doing.

My boss laughed along with the customer, and I mentally stored away this nugget of information for the next time I had a customer whose phone had a lot of faults.

I didn't have to wait too long for an irate customer to appear only a few weeks later with a phone that was so riddled with faults, we just could not figure out the central problem.

"It must be a 'Monday morning' phone," I remarked.

The customer's face reddened and he began spluttering, "What do you mean a 'Monday morning' phone? I was told these were high quality precision engineered in a factory!"

He wanted to speak to my boss. Who was not very happy when he heard what I had said.

The mistake I had made was to answer by rote with a solution that had pleased a completely different type of customer, when what I should have done was listen to what this customer was actually saying to me and by listening, recognizing what was important to that particular customer and using that knowledge to focus on the issue from his point of view.

Calming Down Your Customer

It can be difficult to remove your feelings from a situation when your customer is exploding in anger. After all, we can certainly ignore a jibe or two – and we can continue to try to bring the focus of the disagreement to bear on the product rather than the person – but what happens if the customer's anger just doesn't let up?

This very simple technique will help calm your customer: repeat their words back to them. Not the angry ones, but the ones you have gathered are at the root of the problem when you were actively listening.

By repeating those words back in sentences such as "I understand that you feel the product should do X, when in fact it is doing Y," or "I agree that this should have been delivered to you on Monday and that by not receiving it until Thursday it has caused you considerable inconvenience," you are showing the customer that you are listening to him and are focusing on the root of the problem. You are coming across as someone who is taking responsibility for the issue.

By adopting this manner with the customer, you come across as calm – not defensive or unwilling to see the customer's point of view.

Now it's time for the only emotion that should enter this exchange of views: empathy.

You'll know when your client has shown signs of understanding that you are listening and that they are being heard, when they are

- no longer shouting or using a raised voice
- no longer trying to interrupt you
- nodding in agreement with what you are saying
- looking towards the floor rather than straight in your face

At this point you should use some open bodied gestures of supplication – such as displaying open palms, lowering your shoulders – which may have become hunched up with stress, and mimicking your customer's stance.

Don't look at the floor, or over your customer's shoulder. Look them straight in the eye. No one trusts someone who won't look then in the eye when speaking with them.

Direct eye contact is not aggressive when backed up by non-aggressive body language. It creates the perfect balance that says you are in empathy with them, but are retaining your authority.

As humans we are natural mimics – by using these techniques you are creating a bond with your customer, even though they may not realize it.

There's no need to go buying a lot of body language books, and often that's counterintuitive because if you are trying to remember and act out newly learned techniques your behavior doesn't seem natural - it will have the opposite effect of making your customer feel uneasy in your company.

It's far better to master these few techniques until they become a natural part of your behavior and use them to maximum effect.

Take responsibility for the situation by apologizing. Don't start shifting blame to the company or your customer. You are your company's ambassador and as such represent them in customer service.

Solve the Problem

Offer suggestions as to how you could best clear up the situation. This works best when you become personally involved in the solution. Don't turn to a nearby staff member and start delegating (at least not in front of your customer).

You may not be able to solve the problem. Maybe the problem occurred in the past and there's nothing you can do about it right now that will change the unfortunate result for your customer.

If that's the case, just ask the customer how they feel you can resolve the issue best.

Are they adamant that you can't do anything now and that it's all spilled milk? Then start thinking outside the box. Are you in a position to offer a voucher or coupon – some kind of discount that the customer will appreciate and feel is some kind of compensation for the loss of their time or money.

Don't Delay

When given the chance to rectify the situation, don't delay in putting it into action. Taking immediate action will close the wound faster and minimize the fallout. Your customer will be glad that it was dealt with promptly and so will you be.

Follow Up

Nothing shows genuine concern more than taking the time to follow up with your customer *after* the issue has been resolved. It might be just to ask if they are still happy with the problem resolution or if they require further assistance.

If you haven't already offered one, this may be the perfect time for that discount coupon.

Create a Policy

Remember that a policy is not a strict rule to be rattled off the next time a customer makes the same complaint. It's a guideline. Something to help shape your response next time a similar issue occurs.

The best staff training possible is real life experience. That doesn't mean to say you can't retell a few stories to help give employees a frame of reference for their actions.

Don't let a difficult customer experience become just another story to tell around the water cooler – use it to shape a better business, and reduce future stress by solving issues in advance.

Use the Internet

Today's society makes a lot of use of the Internet for communication. This is the perfect opportunity for you to take your recent customer experience and create a step-by-step solution to add to your company FAQ page so that other customers are more aware of how to avoid the same issue – if that's within their power to do so.

By educating your future customers, you also avoid similar difficult customers in the future.

The Common Denominator (It Might Just Be You)

This might sting a little.

Do you end each day with a stress headache after a day of dealing with idiots? Do you find that no one else in your organization does their job properly and that you have to do it for them?

Let me take this a little further. Your boss doesn't recognize the level of work you do (and doesn't understand the job you do). Worse still, your boss is forever kowtowing to your colleagues – the same ones that sit around and do nothing all day.

It might be time to self assess.

If you're the common denominator in this equation – if it's you that has issues with everyone else around you – then it's quite likely it's you that's at fault.

None of us like to think that we're the ones at fault – and that behind our backs, people are talking about us. We don't like to think that maybe we're just not as efficient at our jobs as we think we are.

When every customer is a difficult customer, it's time for some hard thinking.

Sometimes we need to look at ourselves as if we are a difficult customer and figure out what it is that's causing our negative behavior. Often, in a business setting, it comes down to a feeling of a lack of control in the workplace.

If that's the case for you, it's important to start being more objective about your position in life.

Maybe you feel like you're "just another employee" in your bosses eyes, or the one people can dump their junk on in the eyes of your colleagues – and quite possibly you feel like you're out on the front line in a war when you are faced by customers.

Remember, that no matter what your boss thinks, when you deal with a customer – you are the ambassador for your business.

No matter what your colleagues think, if you are a good ambassador for your business in the eyes of the customers, you can represent yourself as a professional by providing the kind of customer service that marks people out as great business people.

But if you find yourself dogged by a bad attitude – you're the bad customer. Remember that in modern business, we are each other's customers in terms of business departments and services.

Start looking at how you can help yourself become a better customer. If your world view is influenced by what you do for a living, then maybe it's time for a change.

Stress relief comes in many forms. Unfortunately long and unsocial work hours often result in self medication via cigarettes, alcohol and self destructive behavior.

To gain a more balance mental approach to life, try focusing on a healthy activity like running or yoga. Even weight training or a combat sport will help.

The old adage "a healthy mind in a healthy body" is true.

CONCLUSION

By now you should have a clear insight into customer service and what difference it makes to your business and your peace of mind when you have a clear policy in place to deal with situations based on experience.

You don't have to wait – brainstorm a few bad customer experiences with your colleagues. Ones you or they have had – or had to deal with.

You'll also understand that dealing with difficult customers needn't be something that you must try to avoid at all costs. They provide an opportunity to flex your customer care skills – and you can change a customer's entire attitude by matching their concerns and showing you understand them – both verbally and physically.

Sometimes a difficult customer will even become one of your staunchest advocates when they recognize your tenacity in dealing with their problem.

Adapting a flexible attitude to customer service (ditching any scripts) will help you become a memorable and positive person in the eyes of your customers.

Remember that businesses that stand out, such as Selfridges and Nordstrom, do so because their focus is on providing the best customer care possible.

Don't forget that difficult customers are always going to be a part of any business, but your customer service plan should start way before they get the opportunity to cause you trouble, by planning for pre- and post- sale care for your customers.

Educating your customers on what product suits their needs best and how to get the most effective use from it will help avoid issues at a later date.

What You Need to Internalize

We've talked a lot about customer service, types of customers who you are likely to come across – why they feel aggrieved, and more. But you don't need to carry a copy of your customer care policy book around with you all day.

By simply internalizing 10 key takeaways from this report, you can effectively navigate the difficult customer minefield quite safely.

TOP 10 TAKEAWAYS

While you may be more familiar with the idea of 10 Commandments, not every rule suits every person. So while these 10 key points are going to help you, it's best if you think about how they might be altered to suit your specific situation. That's why they're called The 10 Suggestions.

The 10 Suggestions

1. Pre-empt all customer interaction by educating your customers about their choice of product. Provide as much detailed information as possible and an FAQ so that they understand what they are buying and how to get the best use from it.

2. The Customer is Always Right is not to be believed. We know they are wrong. Sometimes even they know they are wrong. But focus on solving the issue – and ignore the customer's personality.

3. Don't get flustered. Pause – and breathe – before you respond. Distance yourself emotionally from any reaction you feel to the customer on a personal level.

4. Focus on the issue and how it can be solved. Don't shift blame to the customer or your company, but just accept responsibility for fixing what needs to be fixed right here and right now – even if that's your customer's ego.

5. Every brush with a difficult customer provides an opportunity to better educate future customers on how to use your product or service in such a way that they will not experience the same issue.

6. Empathize with customers, and repeat their words back to them so that they can see that you are making an effort to see their point of view. This will calm them down and prevent the issue escalating to unfortunate proportions.

7. Difficult customers can become staunch advocates when they are dealt with in a professional manner, so it's always worth taking the time to care for their needs appropriately.

8. Speed of resolution is your number one tool for issue resolution. The faster you can deal with the issue, the quicker you can get away from a difficult customer – and the more professional you will look in their eyes – that's a win-win situation!

9. Always take responsibility, and never try to shift blame.

10. Finally, customer service is a specialized part of business and taking the time to learn how to administer excellent customer care marks you out as a professional. With that in mind, you need to continue your education by reading and learning from those who have gone before you – like Dale Carnegie.

Printed by Libri Plureos GmbH in Hamburg, Germany